#smartpar ntsdothis

#SmartParentsDoThis

A Parent Handbook on How to Raise Smart Kids

#SmartParentsDoThis: A Parent Handbook on How to Raise Smart Kids
Copyrighted ©2021 by SmartParentsDoThis LLC
Dr. Audrey McKenna Wittenauer
Dr. Karla M Holland
Zabrina M Grigsby MSW

Illustrations copyrighted © 2021 Amara NayBab & Fenny S. Santoso
fennyssantoso@gmail.com

ISBN: 9781949109610
Library of Congress Control Number: 2021930964

Printed in the United States
Anchor Book Press, Ltd
440 W. Colfax Street, Unit 1132
Palatine, IL 60078

Cover Design: Amara NayBab

#SmartParentsDoThis

A Parent Handbook on How to Raise Smart Kids

SmartParentsDoThis, LLC
©

Anchor Book Press · Palatine

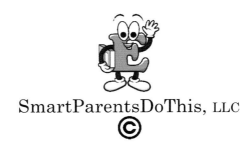

SmartParentsDoThis, LLC
©

Welcome to #SmartParentsDoThis ~ A Parent Handbook on How to Raise Smart Kids.

Congratulations! The very fact that you are reading this book means you are a parent that loves and cares about the future of your children. We are happy that you have chosen our book to lead your family on the road to success. Parenting, as you know, is not for the faint at heart. It is a 24-hour a day job, one that sometimes leaves us tired, stressed, and beaten down. On other days parenting is joyous, filled with laughter and moments of pure happiness. Our goal is to help parents on their journey in raising smart, responsible, and successful children. *#SmartParentsDoThis* will lead you with easy-to-follow steps that will create an environment in your home that will set your children up for success in school and in life.

This book will engage your family in a wonderful experience that will be sure to educate, empower, and elevate families and students alike. It is designed to provide valuable information of what has worked, will work, and is working for parents and caregivers. It will help guide families in learning the skills needed to prepare children for future success through practical parenting tips.

SmartParentsDoThis, LLC is based on more than 50 years of combined experience in education working with students and families to achieve success.

Chapter One~Introduction

#smartparentsdothis

How do we define success?

Success is not the key to happiness. **Happiness** is the key to success. If you love what you are doing, you will be successful.

-Albert Schweitzer
(Schweitzer, n.d.)

We can all agree, as parents we want our children to be successful. Right? What does success look like? Albert Schweitzer says, "Success is not the key to happiness. Happiness is the key to success. If you love what you are doing, you will be successful". This is one definition that goes beyond money, fame, and big toys. The idea that success is doing what you love can cause us to think differently about how we define success.

Take a moment and write your definition of success for your children.

_____
_____
_____
_____
_____

#smartparentsdothis

"I've failed over and over and that is why I succeed."

(Jordan, 2005)

https://www.youtube.com/watch?v=zLYECljmnQs

(Motivating Success, 2012)

If you are able, watch the YouTube video titled, "Famous Failures". It is an inspiring video on persevering no matter how many times you have failed in life. This video mentions well-known people who had failed but kept pressing on until they became successful. It includes people like Michael Jordan. After being cut from his high school basketball team, he went home, locked himself in his room and cried. Albert Einstein wasn't able to speak until he was almost four years old and his teachers said he would "never amount to much." Oprah Winfrey was demoted from her job as a news anchor because she, "Wasn't fit for television." Walt Disney was fired from a newspaper for "lacking imagination" and "having no original ideas." Lionel Messi, at age 11, was cut from his team after being diagnosed with a growth hormone deficiency, which made him smaller in stature than most kids his age. Steve Jobs at 30 years old was left devastated and depressed after being unceremoniously removed from the company he started. Eminem, a high school dropout, whose personal struggles with drugs and poverty culminated in an unsuccessful suicide attempt. Thomas Edison's teacher told him he was, "Too stupid to learn anything" and that he should go into a field where he might succeed by virtue of his pleasant personality. The Beatles were rejected by Decca Recording

Studios, who said, "We don't like their sound; They have no future in show business." Dr. Seuss's first book was rejected by 27 publishers. Abraham Lincoln's fiancé died, he failed in business, had a nervous breakdown, and was defeated in eight elections. "If you've never failed, you've never tried anything new." http://youtu.be/zLYECIjmnQs.

When we talk about success, we must also discuss failure. Why? Because it is through failure that we build character, grit, and perseverance, all traits of successful people. Our children are going to fail. We all do. But the key is to help our kids learn from their failure. Successful people look at their failings and figure out where they went wrong and persevere until they get it right. Children are not born with the ability to process failure. It is our job to teach them. We begin by modeling for them what learning from failure looks like. We ask them questions such as: How could you have done this differently? How did this make you feel? What will you do next time so that you will get a different outcome?

To help us focus our thinking about our children's success let's go through the process of goal setting. On the next page you will see Goals for My Child. There are two copies, feel free to make extra copies if you have more than two children. Goals can be short term or long term. A short-term goal would be to master multiplication facts or memorize the ABC's. An example of a long-term goal (depending on the age of the child) would be to graduate from high school. Take a moment, read through the example, and let's see what kind of goals you can set with your child.

SmartParentsDoThis, LLC

 # GOALS FOR MY CHILD

Child's Name: _____

Goal Statement:

Action Steps:

Goals should be Achievable, Realistic, Specific, and Measurable
Example: My child will memorize sight words by December 12. (Goal set October 1)

Action Steps should show what needs to happen for the goal to be achieved.
Example:
1. My child will study sight words for 20 minutes Monday-Wednesday
2. We will make flash cards for sight words
3. I will test my child on his/her sight words on Thursday
4. When one set of sight words are mastered we will move on to the next set and repeat the process.

SmartParentsDoThis, LLC

★ GOALS FOR MY CHILD ★

Child's Name: _____

Goal Statement:

Action Steps:

Goals should be Achievable, Realistic, Specific, and Measurable
Example: My child will memorize sight words by December 12. (Goal set October 1)

Action Steps should show what needs to happen for the goal to be achieved.
Example:
1. My child will study sight words for 20 minutes Monday-Wednesday
2. We will make flash cards for sight words
3. I will test my child on his/her sight words on Thursday
4. When one set of sight words are mastered we will move on to the next set and repeat the process.

#smartparentsdothis

A beautiful picture of our job...

https://www.youtube.com/watch?v=kZlXWp6vFdE

(De Dominicis, 2014)

If you are able, watch the YouTube video, Derek Redmond -You Raise Me Up. After Derek Redmond tore his hamstring during the 400m semifinal at the 1992 Olympics, his father Jim came out of the stands to help him cross the finish line. While Derek Redmond didn't win a medal at the Olympics, it was his determination to finish that will live forever in the minds of millions. When Redmond got back to his feet after being down and in pain, he showed true courage against adversity as he had to hop on one leg toward the finish line. Each step became more painful than the last, but he would not give up. In tears, with desperation and pain, Derek, was joined by his father Jim. The moment that Redmond crossed the finish line 65,000 spectators rose to a standing ovation. The video became the subject of one of the International Olympic Committee's Celebrate Humanity videos highlighting his 1992 injury, also noting that he and his father finished dead last, but he and his father, finished.

The video is a portrayal of parenting and what our role is in helping our children achieve. As parents, we are to come alongside our child when they fall, help them to get up, and then let them cross the finish line on their own. It is a beautiful picture for ALL of us, no matter how old your child is.

Take a few moments and think about a time your child has struggled or failed. Knowing that failure is necessary for success, how can you use that experience to teach them to persevere? Brainstorm ideas below.

_____
_____
_____
_____
_____
_____
_____
_____

All of this leads to what practical steps can be taken to create a home environment where children can be successful. Families who are intentional about success create School Smart Homes. A School Smart Home is a place where educational success is the number one priority. Parents set a standard or create an environment in a School Smart Home, where children know what is expected of them and where these high expectations become the norm. A School Smart Home is not some unrealistic place in Never Never Land. A School Smart Home is VERY realistic and can be achieved with the easy to remember 6-step system or as we like to call it the 6 Ss. The 6 Ss are Sleep, Space, Supplies, Structure, Supervision, and Support.

#smartparentsdothis

What does a **School Smart Home** look like?

- **S**leep
- **S**pace
- **S**upplies
- **S**tructure
- **S**upervision
- **S**upport

The 6 Ss are simple and easy steps that will set your home up for success in school and for life. Children thrive in environments that are planned and organized because they know what is expected of them, there is no guessing. A School Smart Home provides just that: a place with high expectations, a place where there is freedom to fail, a place where the tools needed for success are easily accessible, and a place where an adult is present to protect and love them.

So let's get started on creating a School Smart Home by digging deeper into the 6 Ss.

Chapter Two ~ SLEEP

The first step in creating a School Smart Home is prioritizing SLEEP. It may sound simple or obvious but sadly too many children, including teenagers, are not getting enough sleep. Read the data from two recent studies on student success and sleep.

#smartparentsdothis

Sleep

- -Too many kids are coming to school tired
- -Studies show sleepiness leads to slipping grades
- -Students with Bs or better get 10-50 minutes more sleep than students with Cs or below

National studies indicate that too many students are coming to school tired. Sleepiness leads to slipping grades. In one National Sleep Foundation experiment, "children were asked to go to bed later than normal for a week, and then were asked to spend no fewer than 10 hours in bed for another week. During the week of later bedtimes, teachers rated these children as having more academic problems and more attention problems (the teachers didn't know they had lost sleep). A lot of parents think their children go to bed early, but even 9:00 pm could be considered a late bedtime for an elementary school child" (National Sleep Foundation, 2018).

"In another study of 1,000 elementary and middle school students, researchers measured children's sleep and school performance and found that one of the best predictors of school failure was children's fatigue (described as being difficult to wake up in the morning and falling asleep during the day). In another study of 3,000 high school students, those who reported higher grades had significantly more sleep time and earlier bedtimes on school nights than those with lower grades. Students with Bs or better went to bed 10-50 minutes earlier than students with Cs and below" (National Sleep Foundation, 2018).

In the past week, write down when your children went to bed and when they got up. How many hours of sleep did they get?

_____

_____

_____

_____

_____

_____

_____

_____

#smartparentsdothis

https://www.youtube.com/watch?v=vljB-ezPufw&t=3os

(Health, 2012)

So let's see how much you know about your child and what his or her growing body needs at different stages. Please take a few moments to answer the Sleep Quiz and then check your answers.

SmartParentsDoThis, LLC
Sleep Quiz

Dream on, dream away........

1. True or False: The amount of recommended sleep decreases as children age.

2. True or False: Teenagers require 6-8 hours of sleep.

3. True or False: Preschoolers require less sleep than elementary age children.

4. True or False: The recommended number of hours of sleep never changes for children.

5. True or False: Children of any age need a consistent bedtime routine.

6. True or False: Children who receive the appropriate amount of sleep receive higher grades.

7. True or False: Sleep apnea only affects adults.

8. True or False: Sleepiness can look like symptoms of ADHD.

9. True or False: Losing 30 - 60 minutes of sleep time doesn't impact a child.

10. True or False: Lack of sleep causes problems with concentration & mood that can lead to behavior problems in class.

(Data from www.sleepfoundation.org)

Sleep Quiz Answers

Dream on, dream away........

1. True - The amount of recommended sleep decreases as children age.

2. False – Teenagers require 6-8 hours of sleep. (True - Teenagers require 8-10 hours of sleep.)

3. False - Preschoolers require less sleep than elementary age children. (True - Preschoolers require more sleep than elementary age children.)

4. False - The recommended number of hours of sleep never changes for children. (True - The recommended number of hours of sleep changes for children.)

5. True - Children of any age need a consistent bedtime routine.

6. True - Children who receive the appropriate amount of sleep receive higher grades.

7. False - Sleep apnea only affects adults. (True - Sleep apnea affects adults and children.)

8. True - Sleepiness can look like symptoms of ADHD.

9. False - Losing 30 - 60 minutes of sleep time doesn't impact a child. (True - Losing 30 - 60 minutes of sleep time does impact a child.)

10. True - Lack of sleep causes problems with concentration & mood that can lead to behavior problems in class.

(Data from www.sleepfoundation.org)

#smartparentsdothis

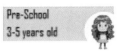

- 10-13 hours of sleep
- 8:00pm bedtime

- 9-11 hours of sleep
- 9:00pm bedtime

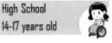

- 8-10 hours of sleep
- 10:00pm bedtime

| Pre-School 3-5 years old | Elementary/Middle 6-13 years old | High School 14-17 years old |

School Smart Homes prioritize sleep because parents know the impact that sleep can make on mood, behavior, attention, and physical growth. The sleep chart above is an easy visual for families to keep track of the various bedtimes that are needed for family members. This chart is also a great tool for children.

The National Sleep Foundation recommends that, "while every child is slightly different in terms of how much sleep he or she may need, most require the amount listed above to be fully rested. Let's note that these are actual sleeping times, not time in bed with an electronic device. So bedtimes are figured on families needing about two hours from alarm to being at school with a wake-up time of 6:00 am. So depending on your particular family you should adjust the times accordingly" (National Sleep Foundation, 2018).

Take a moment and decide when your child needs to go to bed. Then look at the Bedtime Routine Chart to help you and your child achieve sleep goals. The first is an example, the second is a blank chart. Perhaps you can include your child in completing this chart, so he or she can have some ownership in these decisions. No matter what you decide, making sure your child gets the appropriate amount of sleep will be the first step in creating a School Smart Home.

SmartParentsDoThis, LLC
BEDTIME ROUTINE CHART
EXAMPLE:
BEDTIME ROUTINE FOR_____

	Pick up all toys.	7:15PM
	Take a bath or shower.	7:30PM
	Brush your teeth.	8:00PM
	Put on your pajamas.	8:15PM
	Use the bathroom before getting into bed.	8:15PM
	Read a book by yourself or to your parent(s).	8:30PM
	Turn off lights and sleep well.	9:00PM

SmartParentsDoThis, LLC
BEDTIME ROUTINE CHART

BEDTIME ROUTINE FOR_____

SmartParentsDoThis, LLC
BEDTIME ROUTINE CHART

BEDTIME ROUTINE FOR_____

Chapter Three ~ SPACE

#smartparentsdothis

- ✓ Sleep
- **SPACE**
- Supplies
- Structure
- Supervision
- Support

SPACE, so what does that mean? School Smart Homes have a designated homework space for children. Smart parents provide a quiet, uninterrupted area where the child can focus. For young children, it might mean clearing the kitchen table and quieting the home to focus on school work with the parent close by to provide assistance. For older children this might be a desk in a quiet area of the home. The floor in front of the TV is NOT a good homework spot. Providing a designated space for homework sends a clear message and sets the expectation that school is important in your home.

This step in creating a School Smart Home is instrumental in creating an environment that is conducive to learning. When children see a parent create or designate areas of the home specifically for learning that sends a powerful message about the priorities of the home. Specific spaces for learning negate any confusion for children about the importance of education and expectations.

Where might you create spaces for learning in your home? Brainstorm with your children which places in your home would be good for them to concentrate on schoolwork.

_____

_____

_____

_____

_____

_____

_____

_____

Chapter Four ~ SUPPLIES

#smartparentsdothis

- Sleep
- Space
- **SUPPLIES**
- Structure
- Supervision
- Support

So after you designate a space for homework, you need to gather the needed SUPPLIES for your child. Smart parents plan and prepare in advance so that their children have everything needed to succeed.

The easiest way to provide these supplies is to create a Homework Caddy. These supplies stay in the homework space so when your children go to study, everything they need is easily within their reach. You can buy a plastic caddy like those shown in the pictures at a Dollar Store. Fill the Homework Caddy with the supplies your child may need, paper, markers, crayons, scissors, ruler, sticky notes, highlighters, pens, pencils, glue, etc.

#smartparentsdothis

Supplies

Homework Caddies

Another fun way to set the tone of your School Smart Home is to have your children help make the homework caddy. Families who engage in this simple, yet effective activity are setting the expectation of success within their home. In addition, it helps the child feel part of the process which creates buy-in and success.

Remember you can be as creative as you'd like to be with this set up. It can be simple or complex; you and your child decide. Creating this useful tool for home also stimulates great dialogue with your child. You enter his/her world and better understand their ability to analyze and reason as they justify the need for or the lack of need for the various items.

The next page has a suggested shopping list and directions to create your own Homework Caddy.

SmartParentsDoThis, LLC
List of Supplies for a Homework Caddie

Elementary School Age Student	Middle/High School Age Student
Colored Pencils	Calculator (Scientific; this remove the excuse of having to use cell phone for homework)
Crayons	Colored Pencils
Erasers	Correction Tape/White Out
Glue Stick/Bottle of Glue	Glue Stick/Bottle of Glue
Markers	Highlighters (3 different colors)
Pencils/Pens (be sure to include "red" ink for editing	Post-it Notes
Ruler	Markers
Scissors (safe age appropriate)	Index Cards
Cups to match the number of categorized items you have (i.e. 1 cup for pencils, 1 cup for pens, etc.)	Flash Drive/Google Doc (Here is an opportunity for you to learn from your child.)
Caddy	Pens/Pencils (be sure to include "red" ink for editing)
	Ruler/Protractor
	Staple Remover
	Stapler
	Tape
	Cups to match the number of categorized items you have (i.e. 1 cup for highlighters, I cup for pens/pencils, etc.)
	Caddy

Chapter Five ~ STRUCTURE

#smartparentsdothis

- ✓ Sleep
- ✓ Space
- ✓ Supplies
- · **STRUCTURE**
- · Supervision
- · Support

Your children are getting the correct amount of sleep, you've provided the space for homework, and the needed supplies, so now what? As parents, you have to determine how all of this is going to look, or in other words, what is the STRUCTURE of your home. There is no right or wrong answer for this, it's simply what works best for your family. However, you need to decide on what the structure of your evenings will look like. For example, will your children come home, have a snack, and begin working on homework from 5:00-6:00 while you make dinner? Or will your children play after school, have dinner, and then work on homework until bedtime? The point is that as parents you must decide what will work best for your home and child. It might even look differently for each child. Some children just naturally like to come home and get started on homework and have the rest of the night to themselves. Others need to relax from being at school all day, play and eat before they can settle down again to do homework. No matter how you slice it, you as the parent must determine what the expectation in your home will be.

Let's say you determine that dinner is 5:30-6:00 and between 6:00-7:00 is homework time in your house. That means you will have to turn off the TVs, video games, tablets, etc. and set the expectation that everyone in your house will be working on something academic for that hour. If your children don't have an hour's worth of homework, a good practice is to tell kids they can read when they are finished, play a board game with you and/or their siblings, draw, do puzzles, or some other constructive activity, as long as it doesn't involve a screen of any kind. Again, this is setting the expectation in your home that you are about education and providing opportunities for success. It's amazing what kids can accomplish when you stick to your expectations and force them to use their imaginations.

To help you achieve the structure that will work best for your School Smart Home use Our After School Schedule. This is a graphic organizer designed to help you structure your evening. The first page is an example of how a family could organize their after-school time. The second page is a blank copy for you to use with your family. Again this is an excellent opportunity to discuss with your children and hear their thoughts. Smart parents listen to their children's ideas which leads to buy in for the high expectations of your School Smart Home.

SmartParentsDoThis, LLC

Our Afterschool Schedule
Example

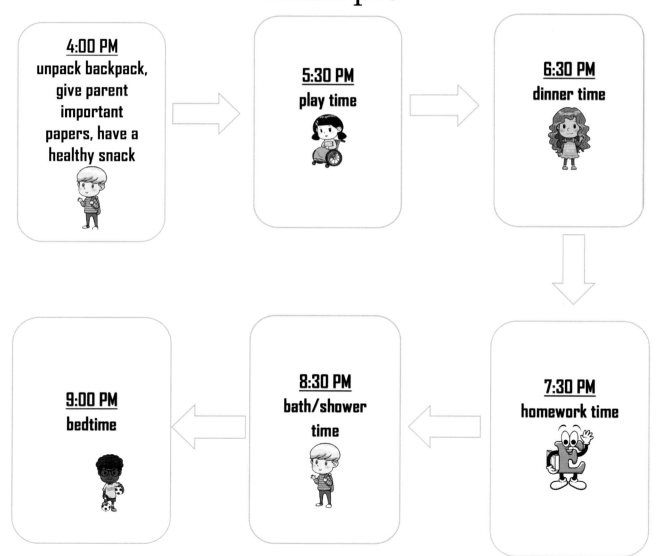

4:00 PM
unpack backpack, give parent important papers, have a healthy snack

5:30 PM
play time

6:30 PM
dinner time

7:30 PM
homework time

8:30 PM
bath/shower time

9:00 PM
bedtime

SmartParentsDoThis, LLC

Our Afterschool Schedule

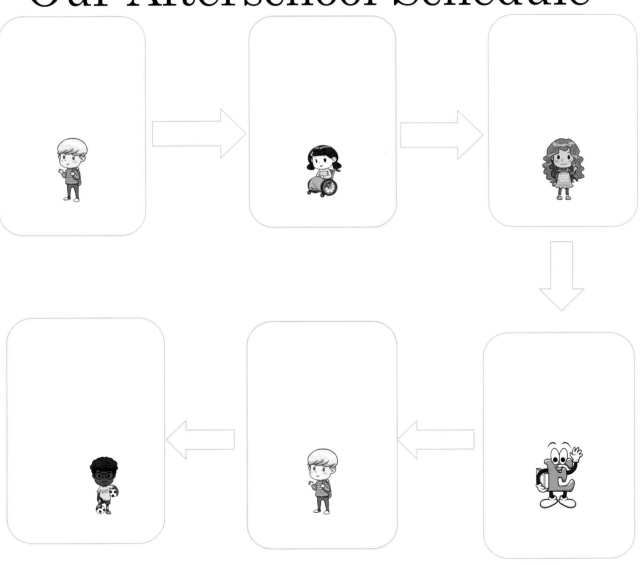

SmartParentsDoThis, LLC

Our Afterschool Schedule

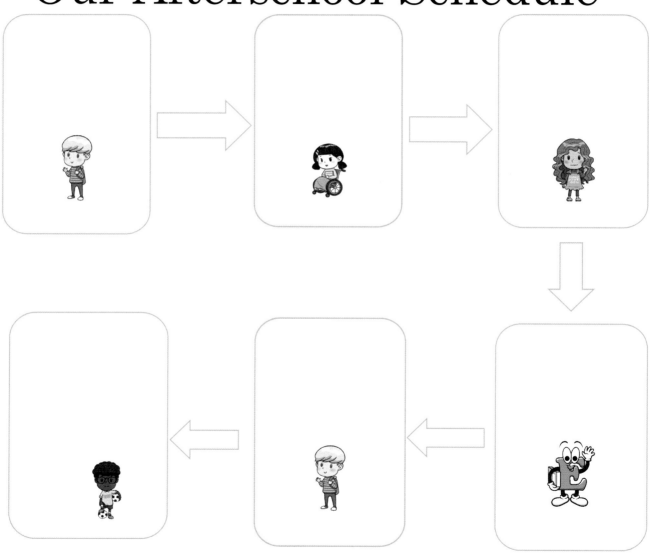

#smartparentsdothis

- ✓ **S**leep
- ✓ **S**pace
- ✓ **S**upplies
- · **STRUCTURE**
- · **S**upervision
- · **S**upport

While we are talking about the structure of your School Smart Home, meal time is something to consider. Research shows that the act of families sitting down and having a meal together is an even more powerful predictor of high achievement scores than time spent in school, doing homework, or playing sports. Family meals are also linked with lowering a host of risky teenage behaviors that parents fear such as smoking, drinking, drug use, and sexual activity. Of course, during these meals, parents are engaged, and no electronic devices are allowed at the table. The real power of family meals lies in their ability to further strengthen relationships. If parents sit in silence, yell at each other, or scold their children, family dinner won't provide any benefits (Delistraty, 2014). Meals can be the perfect chance for a family to talk. With so many activities, work, and school, it is often the only opportunity families have quality time together to communicate. There's nothing magical about sharing tacos on Tuesday. However breakfast, lunch, or dinner may be the one time of the day that children can share a positive experience, tell a joke, or a parent can talk about their day. All of these small moments will create stronger relationships when you are away from the table. Smart parents are able to hear what is really on their children's heart and provide support when needed. Children who have positive and healthy relationships as well as meaningful dialogue with their parents tend to be more successful.

Getting the conversation started that can involve everyone during mealtime can be challenging. SmartParentsDoThis, LLC has created entertaining conversation starters to help families get the fun started. *SmartParentsDoThis ~ Let's Talk Cards* are an easy way to help your family bond, discuss difficult topics, and allow your children to know you are there to listen, support, and guide them to be successful students.

To purchase, visit our website at www.smartparentsdothisllc.com

Chapter Six ~ SUPERVISION

#smartparentsdothis

- ✓ Sleep
- ✓ Space
- ✓ Supplies
- ✓ Structure
- **SUPERVISION**
- Support

School Smart Homes are places where there is SUPERVISION. What is Supervision? It is pretty straightforward. Supervision means the act of monitoring someone or something. Smart parents supervise their children. For the most part children will not automatically want to sit down and work hard on homework, but they will when they know they are being supervised. Again, in School Smart Homes, parents are present and involved in school related activities. Supervision provides accountability which leads to success. What it doesn't mean is that you have to know how to do third grade math, rather you are present to make sure a real effort is being given. If the child is truly stuck, then you can intervene and/or provide the teacher with a quick note or email telling the teacher where your child is having problems. Children with structure and supervision thrive, they may not admit it, but they want it.

Supervision means you will have to monitor the clock, reminding children what time it is, what they need to do next, and to keep the pace moving. You will have to get them to bed on time. Yes, at times it will seem like herding cats, but it is not a losing battle! Keep going, you are doing the hard work of #smartparentsdothis. You will have to be the bad guy that turns off the TV, collects electronic devices at night, and monitors homework hour, but eventually, and we do mean eventually, your children will get on board. Smart parents know that in order for children to be successful they must supervise them.

#smartparentsdothis

https://www.youtube.com/watch?v=mzmXK5XFMOI

(Children of Alabama, 2014)

Electronic Device Contract
- Restricts electronics during mealtimes
- Restricts electronics from bedrooms
- Parents supervise the selection of what is being watched and played

In talking about supervision, we must discuss the use of electronics. We discussed earlier that homework hour is a great time to be an electronic free zone. According to the American Academy of Pediatrics, today's children spend on average 7-8 hours a day with different electronics including cell phones, tablets, computers, and television. This contributes to a lack of sleep and leads to lower academic performance (Children of Alabama, 2014).

If you are able, watch the video Kids and Electronic Devices on YouTube.

The effects of overuse of electronics leads to childhood obesity, limited social interactions, behavioral problems, addictions, and more. Yuck! So again, as smart parents you must supervise electronics. This might mean that your family sets up an Electronic Use Plan. Typically an Electronic Use Plan limits electronic use during mealtime, homework time, and restricts electronics from children's bedrooms.

For families with younger children we have created a tool to assist with the issue of screen time. It is called Electronic Device (ED) Dollars. This is an easy way to monitor the use of electronics in your home and in the process children learn how to become productive members of your household by doing simple chores or tasks.

We have included a blank ED Dollars so you can customize the activities to fit your home. Two copies are provided to help parents tailor to meet the needs of children who are not close in age. Feel free to copy the chart to hang on the fridge.

SmartParentsDoThis, LLC
Electronic Device "ED" Dollars
EXAMPLE:

Activities	ED Dollar Amounts
1. Load Dishwasher/Wash Dishes	2 ED Dollars
2. Empty Dishwasher/Dry and Put Dishes Away	2 ED Dollars
3. Do a load of laundry	1 ED Dollar
4. Fold a load of laundry	1 ED Dollar
5. Vacuum	1 ED Dollar Per Room
6. Put away groceries	1 ED Dollar
7. Parent's choice	1 ED Dollar
8. Play with siblings	2 ED Dollars
9. Clean your room	4 ED Dollars
10. Read a book for 30 minutes	3 ED Dollars
11. Take dog for a walk	2 ED Dollars

1 ED Dollar = 30 minutes of screen time, one episode of TV show, one movie or trade in 20 ED Dollars for $10 real dollars.

SmartParentsDoThis, LLC
Electronic Device "ED" Dollars

Activities	ED Dollar Amounts
1.	__ ED Dollars
2.	__ ED Dollars
3.	__ ED Dollar
4.	__ ED Dollar
5.	__ ED Dollar
6.	__ ED Dollar
7.	__ ED Dollar
8.	__ ED Dollars
9.	__ ED Dollars
10.	__ ED Dollars
11.	__ ED Dollars

1 ED Dollar = _____ minutes of screen time, 1 episode of TV show, a movie or trade in _____ ED Dollars for $_____ real dollars.

Electronic Device "ED" Dollars

Activities	ED Dollar Amounts
3.	__ ED Dollars
4.	__ ED Dollars
3.	__ ED Dollar
4.	__ ED Dollar
5.	__ ED Dollar
6.	__ ED Dollar
7.	__ ED Dollar
8.	__ ED Dollars
9.	__ ED Dollars
10.	__ ED Dollars
11.	__ ED Dollars

1 ED Dollar = _____ minutes of screen time, 1 episode of TV show, a movie or trade in _____ ED Dollars for $_____ real dollars.

#smartparentsdothis

- ✓ Sleep
- ✓ Space
- ✓ Supplies
- ✓ Structure
- · **SUPERVISION**
- · Support

Supervision also includes supervising what children are watching and playing on devices. Let's talk for a few moments about the content of what our children are watching. Do you monitor the TV shows and movies your children watch? Do you know what kinds of video games they are playing? Or what kinds of video clips they are viewing on YouTube? If you are not certain, now is the time to find out. Perhaps begin by asking your children what games and shows they are watching. Maybe sit down with them and watch them play their game or their show.

Smart parents supervise how much time their child spends on electronics and monitors what they are watching on their screens. It is ok to tell children no, this show or that video game is not acceptable in our home. Or this is for older children. Again, you as the smart parent are setting the expectations for your School Smart Home. Your children may put up a fight, but hang tough, you are doing the right thing!

Chapter Seven ~ SUPPORT

#smartparentsdothis

✓ **S**leep
✓ **S**pace
✓ **S**upplies
✓ **S**tructure
✓ **S**upervision
· **SUPPORT**

"Unconditional Love is our birthright, not judgment or condemnation, and there's nothing we need to do to earn it. This is simply who and what we are."

(Moornjani, n.d.)

Last but certainly not least is SUPPORT. Smart parents do all of the things we have discussed through love and support. One could argue that without love and support the other steps will not make a difference. Children are sooo very good at seeing genuineness and calling out fakeness or hypocrisy.

One of the best ways to show children that you love them is to listen to them, know what they like and don't like, hear their funny stories, play games with them, etc. To help facilitate these kinds of discussions and create meaningful dialogue with your child we have created a tool called Three Things. There are 2 copies available: a parent version and a student version. Take turns writing down your answers and share them with each other. Your children will love hearing what you think about them!

SmartParentsDoThis, LLC
Three Things - Parent Version

Three things I like MOST about my child:

    1. _____

    2. _____

    3. _____

Three things I like MOST about ME:

    1. _____

    2. _____

    3. _____

Three things I want my child to accomplish this year:

    1. _____

    2. _____

    3. _____

Three dreams I have for my child for the future:

    1. _____

    2. _____

    3. _____

SmartParentsDoThis, LLC
Three Things - Parent Version

Three things I like MOST about my child:

1. _____

2. _____

3. _____

Three things I like MOST about ME:

1. _____

2. _____

3. _____

Three things I want my child to accomplish this year:

1. _____

2. _____

3. _____

Three dreams I have for my child for the future:

1. _____

2. _____

3. _____

Three Things - Child Version

Three things I like MOST about my parent (Mom, Dad, Granny):

    1. _____

    2. _____

    3. _____

Three things I like MOST about ME:

    1. _____

    2. _____

    3. _____

Three things I want to accomplish this year:

    1. _____

    2. _____

    3. _____

Three dreams I have for the future:

    1. _____

    2. _____

    3. _____

SmartParentsDoThis, LLC
Three Things - Child Version

Three things I like MOST about my parent (Mom, Dad, Granny):

    1. _____

    2. _____

    3. _____

Three things I like MOST about ME:

    1. _____

    2. _____

    3. _____

Three things I want to accomplish this year:

    1. _____

    2. _____

    3. _____

Three dreams I have for the future:

    1. _____

    2. _____

    3. _____

#smartparentsdothis

Easy ways to show support and love:
- Have family dinners regularly
- Play together
- Say "I love you" for no reason
- Cook together, read together
- Watch movies together
- Say thank you to them

Everything we have talked about will be pointless if it is not backed up with Support and Love. On the chart you can see a few easy ways to show kids love and support. Spending quality time with your kids shows them you care about and are interested in their lives. To help with this we have created a fun activity called How Plugged-In Are You to Your Child? You and your child take turns answering the questions and share your answers. It's a fun way to find out what your kids are thinking!

SmartParentsDoThis, LLC
How Plugged-In Are You to Your Child???

Answer the questions below then compare answers with your child.

1. Without looking, describe what your child is wearing?

2. What is the last movie your child saw? What was his or her opinion of the movie?

3. Name at least one item that you would find under your child's bed.

4. When was the last time your child cried? Why?

5. What would your child say he or she is most stressed about?

6. What is your child's favorite subject in school?

7. If your child had $20 to spend today, how would he or she spend it?

8. What would your child say was the best moment of his or her life?

9. What is the LAST name of your child's best friend? What are the names of his or her parents?

10. What is your child's most prized possession?

SmartParentsDoThis, LLC
How Plugged-In Are You to Your Child???

Answer the questions below then compare answers with your child.

1. Without looking, describe what your child is wearing?

2. What is the last movie your child saw? What was his or her opinion of the movie?

3. Name at least one item that you would find under your child's bed.

4. When was the last time your child cried? Why?

5. What would your child say he or she is most stressed about?

6. What is your child's favorite subject in school?

7. If your child had $20 to spend today, how would he or she spend it?

8. What would your child say was the best moment of his or her life?

9. What is the LAST name of your child's best friend? What are the names of his or her parents?

10. What is your child's most prized possession?

Answer the questions below then be prepared to share your answers with your parent(s).

1. Describe what you are wearing at this very moment?

2. What is the last movie you saw? What was your opinion of the movie?

3. Name at least one item that you would find under your bed.

4. When was the last time you cried? Why?

5. What are you most stressed about at this time?

6. What is your favorite subject in school?

7. If you had $20 to spend today, how would you spend it?

8. What would you say is the best moment of your life?

9. What is the LAST name of your best friend? What are the names of his or her parents?

10. What is your most prized possession?

Answer the questions below then be prepared to share your answers with your parent(s).

1. Describe what you are wearing at this very moment?

2. What is the last movie you saw? What was your opinion of the movie?

3. Name at least one item that you would find under your bed.

4. When was the last time you cried? Why?

5. What are you most stressed about at this time?

6. What is your favorite subject in school?

7. If you had $20 to spend today, how would you spend it?

8. What would you say is the best moment of your life?

9. What is the LAST name of your best friend? What are the names of his or her parents?

10. What is your most prized possession?

We have also included 10 Ways to Love a Child. These are really great phrases to use. Words are so powerful; we can tear down or build up our children with our word choices. Choose two or three of these to use this week. Watch how your children blossom when they begin to hear these encouraging and affirming words spoken to them!

If you like these check out, LOVE NOTES. Behind every smart kid is a smart and supportive parent! Let them know you love them by leaving little love notes in your child's lunch box, at their home study area, or on their pillow. Each pack contains 36 notes to choose from with encouraging messages, all you have to do is sign your name. We also included four blank notes for you to create your own personalized message.

To purchase visit www.smartparentsdothisllc.com

#smartparentsdothis

✓ **S**leep
✓ **S**pace
✓ **S**upplies
✓ **S**tructure
✓ **S**upervision
· **SUPPORT**

Another fun activity, Kid Coupons and Parent Coupons. Be creative with how you might use this activity in your home. One example might be to give each child a copy of the Kid Coupons and tell them they can use these however they would like. While at the same time, you as the parent use the Parent Coupons and randomly give out coupons as you see fit. It will be fun to see how these small coupons will engage children and parents in laughter and love. When your home is happy, your children are more successful. We included a blank coupon so you can modify privileges to fit your family and your children's needs.

Feel free to make extra copies of coupons for your family.

SmartParentsDoThis, LLC
Kid Coupons

This card is good for 1 meal made by me! I love pizza! To: _____ From: _____	This card is good for making your bed 1 time by me! Make it perfect! To: _____ From: _____
This card is good for me doing the dishes 1 time! Wash Away! To: _____ From: _____	This card is good for 1 time for me to fold the towels! Perfect Folds! To: _____ From: _____
This card is good for me sweeping the floor 1 time! Sweep, sweep! To: _____ From: _____	This card is good for one 10-minute talk with me Let's Talk! To: _____ From: _____
This card is good for me to feed the animals 1 time! Feeding Time! To: _____ From: _____	This card is good for me to dust 1 time! Perfect Folds! To: _____ From: _____

SmartParentsDoThis, LLC
Kid Coupons

This card is good for 1 meal made by me!

I love pizza!

To: _____
From: _____

This card is good for making your bed 1 time by me!

Make it perfect!

To: _____
From: _____

This card is good for me doing the dishes 1 time!

Wash Away!

To: _____
From: _____

This card is good for 1 time for me to fold the towels!

Perfect Folds!

To: _____
From: _____

This card is good for me sweeping the floor 1 time!

Sweep, sweep!

To: _____
From: _____

This card is good for one 10-minute talk with me

Let's Talk!

To: _____
From: _____

This card is good for me to feed the animals 1 time!

Feeding Time!

To: _____
From: _____

This card is good for me to dust 1 time!

Perfect Folds!

To: _____
From: _____

SmartParentsDoThis, LLC

Parent Coupons

NO CHORES FOR A DAY!

To: _____
From: _____

CHOOSE A MOVIE OR TV SHOW!

To: _____
From: _____

PICK YOUR FAVORITE CEREAL AT THE STORE!

To: _____
From: _____

PLAY ON THE COMPUTER FOR 30 MINUTES!

To: _____
From: _____

STAY UP FOR 30 MINUTES PAST YOUR BEDTIME THIS WEEKEND!

To: _____
From: _____

TRIP TO THE DOLLAR STORE TO PICK OUT SOMETHING SPECIAL!

To: _____
From: _____

CHOOSE WHAT'S FOR DINNER ONE NIGHT THIS WEEK!

To: _____
From: _____

30 MINUTES OF 1 ON 1 TIME WITH PARENT(S) FOR AN ACTIVITY!

To: _____
From: _____

SmartParentsDoThis, LLC

Parent Coupons

NO CHORES FOR A DAY!

To: _____
From: _____

CHOOSE A MOVIE OR TV SHOW!

To: _____
From: _____

PICK YOUR FAVORITE CEREAL AT THE STORE!

To: _____
From: _____

PLAY ON THE COMPUTER FOR 30 MINUTES!

To: _____
From: _____

STAY UP FOR 30 MINUTES PAST YOUR BEDTIME THIS WEEKEND!

To: _____
From: _____

TRIP TO THE DOLLAR STORE TO PICK OUT SOMETHING SPECIAL!

To: _____
From: _____

CHOOSE WHAT'S FOR DINNER ONE NIGHT THIS WEEK!

To: _____
From: _____

30 MINUTES OF 1 ON 1 TIME WITH PARENT(S) FOR AN ACTIVITY!

To: _____
From: _____

SmartParentsDoThis, LLC

Parent Blank Coupons

To: _____
From: _____

To: _____
From: _____

To: _____
From: _____

To: _____
From: _____

To: _____
From: _____

To: _____
From: _____

To: _____
From: _____

To: _____
From: _____

Chapter Eight ~ Review

Reviewing the 6's
- **S**leep
- **S**pace
- **S**upplies
- **S**tructure
- **S**upervision
- **S**upport

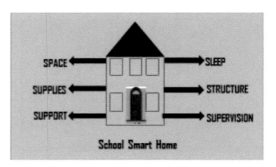

The School Smart Home diagram is a visual reminder of everything we have discussed. Each of the 6 Ss are simple and effective ways for your family to begin the journey toward success. You as a smart parent are capable of setting high expectations for success in your home. There may be a short period of adjustment for your family and perhaps even some pushback but hold the line because your children need and desire the success you will be fostering. Review the 6 Ss as needed, make adjustments as you see fit, and remember you know your children best. Keep doing the hard work of raising successful children. Smart parents have the very same qualities that smart children have; grit, perseverance, and the desire to succeed. Remember parenting is a marathon, not a sprint. We wish you much success as you begin creating your own School Smart Home!

We would love to hear from you! Follow us and share your parenting journey!

References

Children of Alabama. (2014). Kids and electronic devices. Retrieved from
    https://www.youtube.com/watch?v=mzmXK5XFM0I

De Dominicis, M. (2014). Derek Redmond's Incredible Olympic Story -
Barcelona 1992 Olympics.
    Retrieved from https://www.youtube.com/watch?v=V93-mOwkw3I

Delistraty, C. (2014). The importance of eating together. The Atlantic.
Retrieved from
    https://www.theatlantic.com/heatlh/archive/2014/07/the-importance-of-
    eating-together/374256/

Health, L. (2012). Are kids getting enough sleep?. Retrieved from
    https://www.youtube.com/watch?v=vIjB-ezPufw&t=30s

Jordan, M. (2005). Driven from within. New York, NY: Atria Books.
Retrieved from
    https://www.brainyquote.com/quotes/michael_jordan_167379

Moornjani, A. (n.d.). (Direct quote). Retrieved from
    https://quotefancy.com/quote/1712065/Anita-Moorjani-Unconditional-
    Love-is-our-birthright-not-judgment-or-condemnation-and

Motivating Success. (2012). Famous failures. Retrieved from
    https://www.youtube.com/watch?v=zLYECIjmnQs

National Sleep Foundation. (2018). Improve your child's school performance
with a good night's sleep. Retrieved from
    https://sleepfoundation.org/

National Sleep Foundation (2018). Sleep quiz. Retrieved from
    https://sleepfoundation.org/

Schweitzer, A. (n.d.). (Direct quote). Retrieved from
    https://www.brainyquote.com/quotes/albert_schweitzer_155988